GRADE
2

SCHOLASTIC

W9-AYN-770

Success With Addition & Subtraction

New York • Toronto • London • Auckland • Sydney
Mexico City • New Delhi • Hong Kong • Buenos Aires

Teaching *Resources*

State Standards Correlations

To find out how this book helps you meet your state's standards, log on to **www.scholastic.com/ssw**

Written by Danette Randolph
Cover design by Ka-Yeon Kim-Li
Interior illustrations by Carol Tiernon
Interior design by Quack & Company

ISBN 978-0-545-20097-4

Introduction

Parents and teachers alike will find **Addition & Subtraction** *to be a valuable learning tool. Children will enjoy completing a wide variety of math activities that are both engaging and educational. Take a look at the Table of Contents and you will feel rewarded providing such a valuable resource for your children.*

Table of Contents

Spell It Out

Add. Complete the puzzle using number words.

Across

1. 5 + 5 = _____

2. 3 + _____ = 7

3. 2 + _____ = 9

6. 6 + 2 = _____

7. _____ + 0 = 1

Down

1. 4 + _____ = 6

2. 2 + _____ = 7

3. _____ + 4 = 10

4. 4 + 5 = _____

5. 5 + _____ = 8

  Finish each number sentence with a number word.

five + two = _____   three + six = _____

Beautiful Bouquets

Subtract. Draw petals to show the difference.

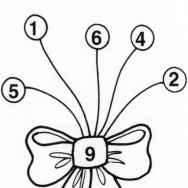

 Color the bows with an even number yellow.
Color the bows with an odd number purple.

Copyright © Scholastic Inc.

Crazy Creatures

Add or subtract. Fill in each missing number.

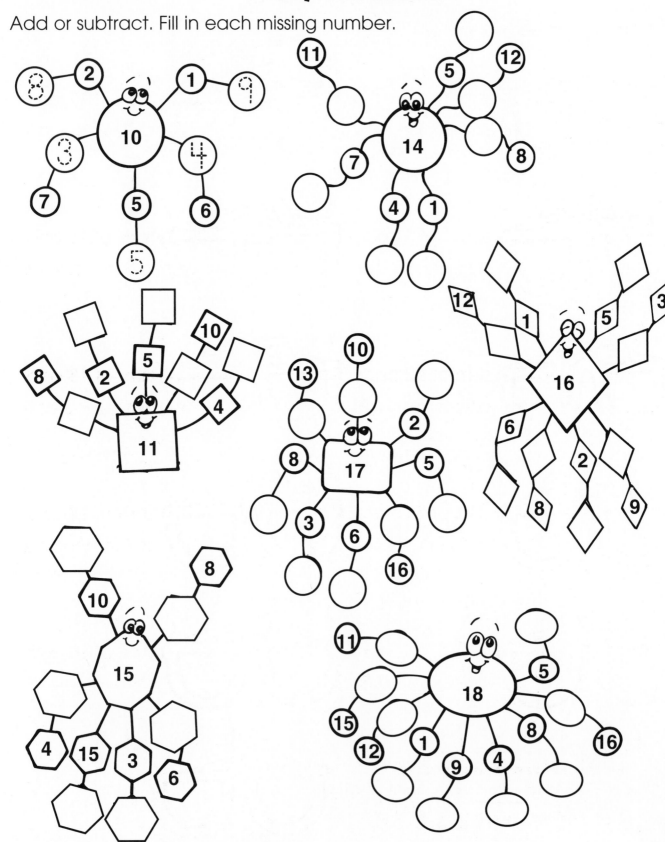

Can You See It?

Write the numbers you see with a . . .

A.  sum of **5** and difference of **1**.

B.  sum of **17** and difference of **7**.

C.  sum of **14** and difference of **2**.

D.  sum of **18** and difference of **4**.

E.  sum of **12** and difference of **2**.

F.  sum of **15** and difference of **9**.

G.  sum of **5** and difference of **3**.

H.  sum of **18** and difference of **2**.

I.  sum of **13** and difference of **5**.

J.  sum of **16** and difference of **6**.

 Make your own number glasses.
sum of _____ and
difference of _____

Counting on Good Manners

Add. Then use the code to write a letter in each oval to find the "good manner" words.

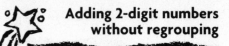

May I have some candy, please?

11 + 10	62 + 31	44 + 34	41 + 5	13 + 31	35 + 43

◯ ◯ ◯ ◯ ◯ ◯

40 + 10	43 + 24	42 + 4	54 + 25	41 + 42

◯ ◯ ◯ ◯ ◯

57 + 2	22 + 3	34 + 32

◯ ◯ ◯

Thank you!

54 + 5	21 + 4	41 + 25	21 + 11	26 + 52

◯ ◯ ◯ ' ◯ ◯

50 + 30	70 + 8	50 + 43	11 + 7	15 + 10	31 + 4	17 + 61

◯ ◯ ◯ ◯ ◯ ◯ ◯

Code

18 C	21 P	25 O	32 R	35 M	44 S	46 A	50 T
59 Y	66 U	67 H	78 E	79 N	80 W	83 K	93 L

Just the Same

Add. Connect the flowers with the same sum.

43
+ 26

18
+ 70

11
+ 34

62
+ 35

13
+ 12

52
+ 36

23
+ 22

51
+ 18

14
+ 11

55
+ 42

 Make matching sums.

+	+		+	+
78	78		54	54

Name _____

Planet Earth

Add.

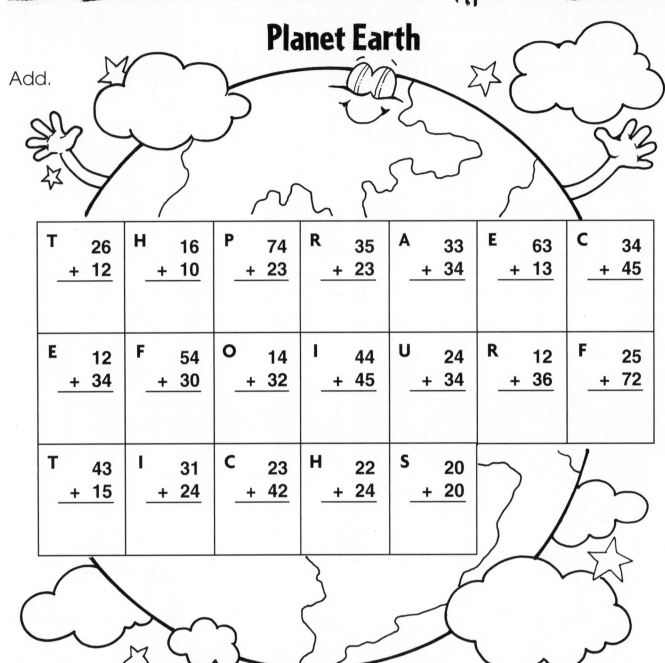

T 26 + 12	**H** 16 + 10	**P** 74 + 23	**R** 35 + 23	**A** 33 + 34	**E** 63 + 13	**C** 34 + 45
E 12 + 34	**F** 54 + 30	**O** 14 + 32	**I** 44 + 45	**U** 24 + 34	**R** 12 + 36	**F** 25 + 72
T 43 + 15	**I** 31 + 24	**C** 23 + 42	**H** 22 + 24	**S** 20 + 20		

For each sum that is an even number, write its letter below in order.

How much of the earth is covered by water?

___ ___ ___ ___ ___ — ___ ___ ___ ___ ___ ___

For each sum that is an odd number, write its letter below in order.

What is the biggest ocean?

___ ___ ___ ___ ___ ___ ___ ___

High Flying

Subtract.

96
− 34

59
− 26

65
− 42

81
− 51

43
− 22

78
− 64

84
− 23

37
− 15

92
− 51

 Color the bird with the smallest number in the ones place red.

Color the bird with the smallest number in the tens place blue.

Color each bird with the same number in the ones and tens place green.

Weather Drops

Subtract. Using the difference in each rain drop, write the weather words in order of their differences from least to greatest by the umbrella handle. Then color your favorite kind of "weather drop" blue.

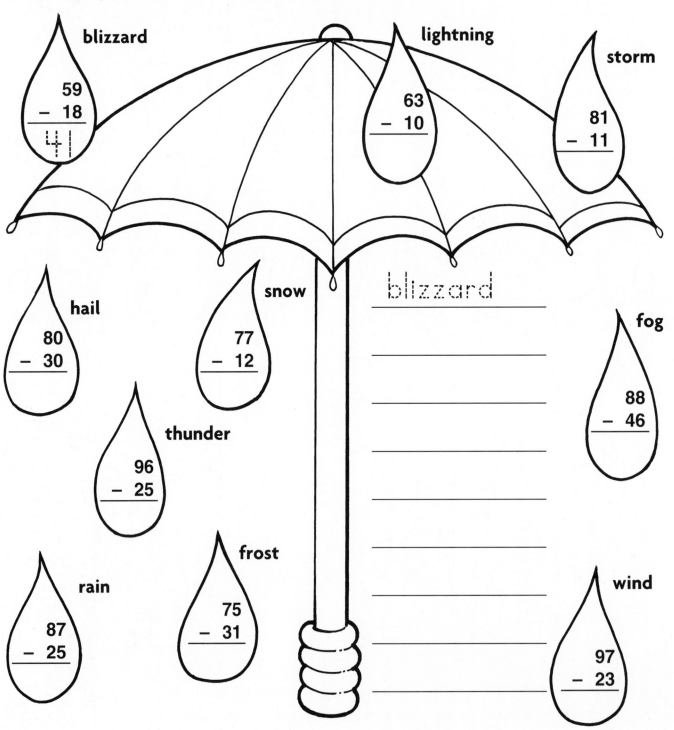

blizzard

$$59 - 18 = 41$$

lightning

$$63 - 10$$

storm

$$81 - 11$$

hail

$$80 - 30$$

snow

$$77 - 12$$

fog

$$88 - 46$$

thunder

$$96 - 25$$

blizzard

rain

$$87 - 25$$

frost

$$75 - 31$$

wind

$$97 - 23$$

Name _____

Animal Families

Subtract.

96 − 42

97 − 12

86 − 43

99 − 14

98 − 55

78 − 24

89 − 22

77 − 34

78 − 11

95 − 63

88 − 56

Color the animals using the color code.

red	blue	purple	yellow	green
32	43	54	67	85

Triple the Fun

Add. Write the sum on each bowl.

 Color bowls with 1, 5, or 8 in the ones place yellow.
Color bowls with 0, 4, or 7 in the ones place pink.
Color bowls with 2, 6, or 9 in the ones place brown.

A Great Catch

Circle each group of 10. Write the number of tens and ones on the chart.
Then write the number on the baseball glove.

tens	ones
1	3

tens	ones

tens	ones

tens	ones

tens	ones

tens	ones

tens	ones

tens	ones

Don't Forget Your Keys

Add. Then follow the clue to find the right key. Write the sum in the key hole.

A.

43
+ 9

87
+ 6

64
+ 8

Find the key with the greatest number in the tens place.

B.

36
+ 5

55
+ 7

29
+ 8

Find the key with the greatest number in the ones place.

C.

14
+ 9

43
+ 7

58
+ 4

Find the key with even numbers in the ones and tens places.

D.

53
+ 7

24
+ 8

75
+ 6

Find the key with 0 in the ones place.

E.

84
+ 6

36
+ 8

67
+ 9

Find the key with the same number in the ones and tens places.

Treasure of a Book

Add. Then color each box with an odd sum to help the boy find his way to the book. Hint: Remember to look in the ones place.

47 + 24	74 + 19	78 + 12	15 + 37
48 + 44	31 + 59	52 + 39	29 + 57	73 + 19
63 + 18	14 + 67	57 + 16	24 + 18	63 + 29
57 + 28	27 + 47	76 + 16	72 + 18	76 + 18
32 + 19	17 + 24	55 + 38	32 + 49	

Name _____

How Do We Get There?

49 miles

32 miles

31 miles

54 miles

MOUNTAINS

13 miles

48 miles

25 miles

17 miles

88 miles

BEACH

10 miles

28 miles

39 miles

Add the distance of each route from the house to the beach.

Route #1   Route #2

_____   _____

_____   _____

_____   _____

+ _____   + _____

_____   _____
   miles   miles

Add the distance of each route from the house to the mountains.

Route #1   Route #2

_____   _____

_____   _____

_____   _____

+ _____   + _____

_____   _____
   miles   miles

Crack the Numbers

Look at the number on each chick. Write the number of tens and ones on the egg. Then trade one ten for ten ones.

Digging Up Bones

Help Daisy find a delicious bone! Subtract.
Circle the answer that goes with each bone.

> is greater than and < is less than

A.

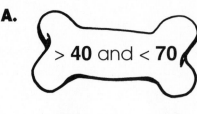

> **40** and < **70**

56	94
− 8	− 5

B.

> **25** and < **55**

87	53
− 8	− 7

C.

> **37** and < **82**

45	81
− 9	− 5

D.

> **74** and < **96**

83	68
− 6	− 9

E.

> **18** and < **49**

57	23
− 9	− 9

F.

> **63** and < **87**

70	75
− 9	− 7

G.

> **16** and < **56**

23	47
− 9	− 8

 Write two subtraction problems on another piece of paper. One answer should match the bone.

> **48** and < **87**

Name _____

First, Next, Last

Subtract. Then number the pictures in order from least to greatest.

A.

```
  64        58        83
- 45      - 19      - 46
```

B.

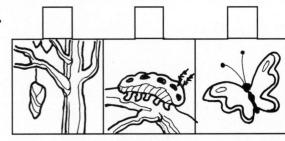

```
  83        24        28
- 75      - 18      - 19
```

C.

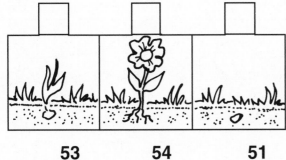

```
  53        54        51
- 25      - 17      - 37
```

D.

```
  88        91        82
- 59      - 53      - 45
```

E.

```
  73        71        76
- 44      - 35      - 28
```

F.

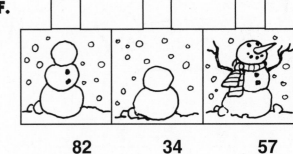

```
  82        34        57
- 64      - 19      - 38
```

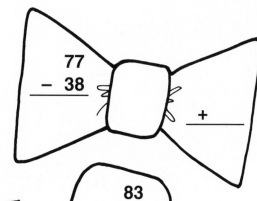

All Tied Up

Subtract. Add to check.

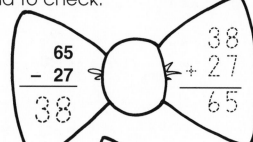

$$\begin{array}{r} 65 \\ -\ 27 \\ \hline 38 \end{array} \qquad \begin{array}{r} 38 \\ +\ 27 \\ \hline 65 \end{array}$$

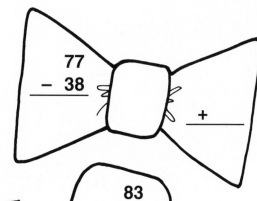

$$\begin{array}{r} 77 \\ -\ 38 \\ \hline \end{array} \qquad \begin{array}{r} + \\ \hline \end{array}$$

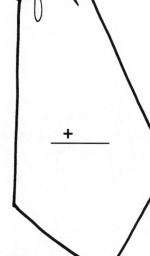

$$\begin{array}{r} 24 \\ -\ 15 \\ \hline \end{array} \qquad \begin{array}{r} + \\ \hline \end{array}$$

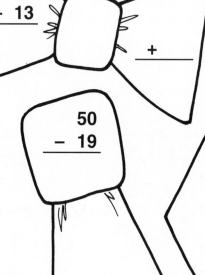

$$\begin{array}{r} 32 \\ -\ 13 \\ \hline \end{array} \qquad \begin{array}{r} + \\ \hline \end{array}$$

$$\begin{array}{r} 83 \\ -\ 49 \\ \hline \end{array} \qquad \begin{array}{r} + \\ \hline \end{array}$$

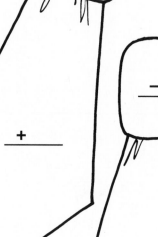

$$\begin{array}{r} 50 \\ -\ 19 \\ \hline \end{array} \qquad \begin{array}{r} + \\ \hline \end{array}$$

$$\begin{array}{r} 46 \\ -\ 29 \\ \hline \end{array} \qquad \begin{array}{r} + \\ \hline \end{array}$$

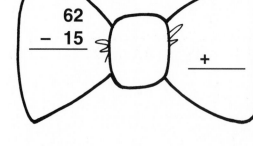

$$\begin{array}{r} 62 \\ -\ 15 \\ \hline \end{array} \qquad \begin{array}{r} + \\ \hline \end{array}$$

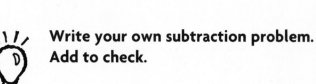

Write your own subtraction problem. Add to check.

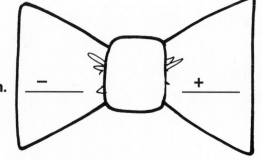

$$\begin{array}{r} - \\ \hline \end{array} \qquad \begin{array}{r} + \\ \hline \end{array}$$

Teenie Tiny Babies

Add or subtract.

U.	42 + 39	**L.**	53 − 48	**N.**	31 + 29	**C.**	74 − 28	**O.**	44 + 46

P.	75 − 37	**H.**	40 − 17	**K.**	27 + 36	**S.**	96 − 48	**A.**	62 − 48

G.	80 − 62	**M.**	55 + 16	**R.**	88 − 19

Write the letter that goes with each number.

I am smaller than your
thumb when I'm born.

 ___ ___ ___ ___ ___ ___ ___ ___
 63   14   60   18   14   69   90   90

I am even smaller.

 ___ ___ ___ ___ ___
 63   90   14   5   14

I am smaller than a bumblebee.

 ___ ___ ___ ___ ___ ___ ___
 90   38   90   48   48   81   71

Since we are so little, we
live right next to our mothers in a safe, warm ___ ___ ___ ___ ___ .
 38   90   81   46   23

Day by Day

Add or subtract. Color each special date on the calendar.

July

Sun.	Mon.	Tues.	Wed.	Thur.	Fri.	Sat.
		1	2	3	4	5
6	7	8	9	10	11	12
13	14	15	16	17	18	19
20	21	22	23	24	25	26
27	28	29	30	31		

A. Camp begins one week after the second Monday. Color this date red.

B. The baseball game is two weeks before the fourth Wednesday. Color this date green.

C. The birthday party is two weeks after the second Saturday. Color this date purple.

D. The swim meet is three weeks before the fifth Tuesday. Color this date blue.

E. The trip to the zoo is one week before the third Sunday. Color this date orange.

F. The picnic is two weeks before the fifth Thursday. Color this date yellow.

G. What date is 14 days after the third Wednesday? Color this date pink.

H. What date is 18 days before the fourth Friday? Color this date brown.

Pizza Vote

Use the circle graph to compare the results of the pizza vote.

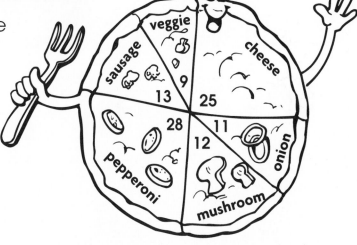

A. How many students voted for pepperoni and cheese in all?

B. How many more students voted for cheese than veggie?

C. How many more students voted for pepperoni than sausage?

D. How many students voted for mushroom and veggie altogether?

E. How many more students voted for mushroom than veggie?

F. How many students voted for sausage and pepperoni in all?

G. How many students voted for veggie, cheese, and mushroom in all?

 Find the total number of students who voted.

Tool Time

Find the sum of the numbers in each tool.

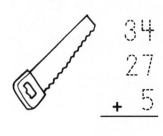

```
  34
  27
+  5
_____
```

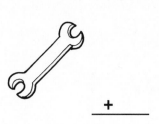

+ _____

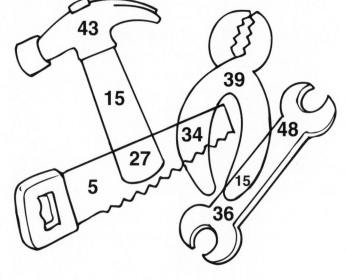

+ _____

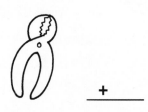

+ _____

A. Write the number found in the 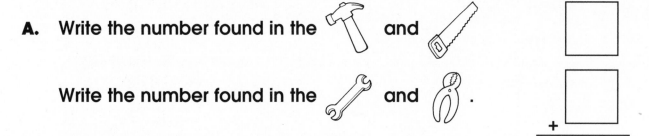 and

Write the number found in the ___ and ___ .

```
┌──────┐
│      │
└──────┘
┌──────┐
│      │
└──────┘
+ _____
```

Find the sum.

B. Find the difference between the largest and smallest numbers in each tool.

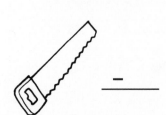 – _____   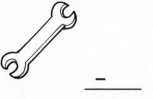 – _____    – _____   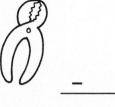 – _____

 On another piece of paper, find the sum of the tools altogether.
Hint: You'll be adding nine numbers.

Powerful Presidents

Add. Color each even sum red to learn about George Washington. Color each odd sum blue to learn about Abe Lincoln. Hint: Look in the ones place.

A. the "Father of the Country"

$$\begin{array}{r} 423 \\ +\ 173 \\ \hline \end{array}$$

B. born in 1809 in Kentucky

$$\begin{array}{r} 384 \\ +\ 611 \\ \hline \end{array}$$

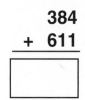

C. sixteenth president

$$\begin{array}{r} 325 \\ +\ 552 \\ \hline \end{array}$$

D. 6 feet 4 inches tall

$$\begin{array}{r} 257 \\ +\ 312 \\ \hline \end{array}$$

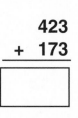

E. born in 1732 in Virginia

$$\begin{array}{r} 101 \\ +\ 561 \\ \hline \end{array}$$

F. studied geography

$$\begin{array}{r} 570 \\ +\ 408 \\ \hline \end{array}$$

G. first president

$$\begin{array}{r} 805 \\ +\ 163 \\ \hline \end{array}$$

H. leader in the Revolutionary War

$$\begin{array}{r} 445 \\ +\ 151 \\ \hline \end{array}$$

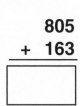

I. loved reading books

$$\begin{array}{r} 609 \\ +\ 290 \\ \hline \end{array}$$

J. leader in the Civil War

$$\begin{array}{r} 314 \\ +\ 183 \\ \hline \end{array}$$

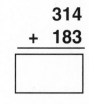

Hundreds of Pumpkins

Regroup tens into hundreds. Remember: 10 tens = 1 hundred. Write the number of hundreds and the number of remaining tens.

27 tens

__2__ hundred

__7__ tens

84 tens

_____ hundreds

_____ tens

93 tens

_____ hundred

_____ tens

71 tens

_____ hundreds

_____ tens

56 tens

_____ hundreds

_____ tens

32 tens

_____ hundreds

_____ tens

49 tens

_____ hundreds

_____ tens

65 tens

_____ hundreds

_____ tens

Write the number.

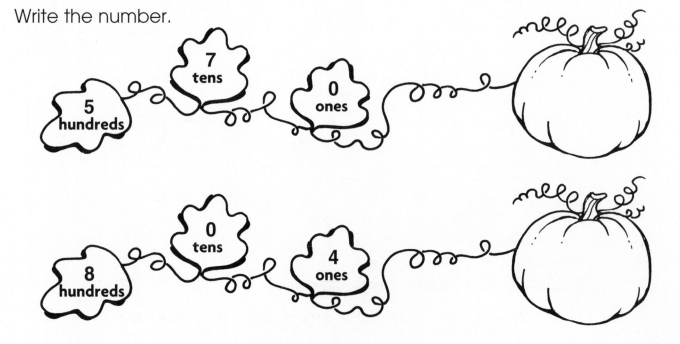

5 hundreds   **7 tens**   **0 ones**

8 hundreds   **0 tens**   **4 ones**

Through the Tunnels

Add. Then trace the mole's path to the top. The mole must travel through tunnels with a zero in the sum.

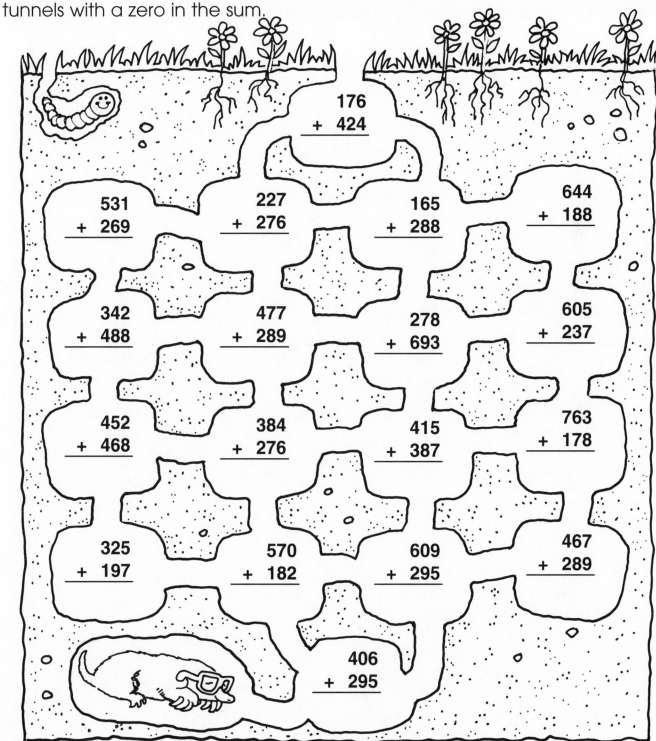

$$176 + 424$$

$$531 + 269$$

$$227 + 276$$

$$165 + 288$$

$$644 + 188$$

$$342 + 488$$

$$477 + 289$$

$$278 + 693$$

$$605 + 237$$

$$452 + 468$$

$$384 + 276$$

$$415 + 387$$

$$763 + 178$$

$$325 + 197$$

$$570 + 182$$

$$609 + 295$$

$$467 + 289$$

$$406 + 295$$

 On another piece of paper, write three more problems that have a zero in the sum.

Sandwich Shop

Menu

hot dog ....$1.53   fruit salad..........$1.90

pbj...................$1.49   veggies & dip ...$1.84

turkey sub.........$1.86   chips ....$ .50

hamburger........$1.72   fries....................$ .65

juice ....$ .84   cupcake...........$1.07

milk...................$ .75   brownie $1.22

shake ....$1.17   cookies ....$ .86

Add.

A.

pbj

chips

milk

brownie   + _____

B.

hamburger

fries

shake   + _____

C.

turkey sub

veggies & dip

juice

cupcake   + _____

D.

hot dog

fruit salad

brownie

juice   + _____

E.

turkey sub

chips

shake   + _____

F.

pbj

cookies

milk   + _____

Easy as 1, 2, 3

Add to find the perimeter of each shape.

A.

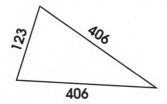

B.

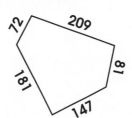

C.

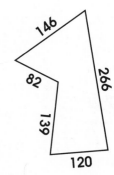

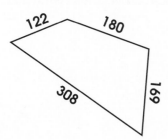

$+$ _____

$+$ _____

D.

E.

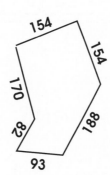

F.

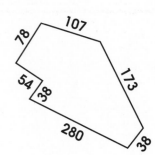

$+$ _____

$+$ _____

$+$ _____

💡 **Color each shape using the code below.**

9 hundreds — orange	4 tens — red	3 ones — purple
6 hundreds — green	7 tens — yellow	8 ones — blue

Count Down

Regroup hundreds to tens. Remember: 1 hundred = 10 tens.

4 hundreds
___ tens

2 hundreds
___ tens

7 hundreds
___ tens

5 hundreds
___ tens

1 hundred
___ tens

9 hundreds
___ tens

8 hundreds
___ tens

3 hundreds
___ tens

The Sun's Family

Draw a line to each matching difference to connect each planet to a fact about it.

Mars

694
− 421

Saturn

935
− 123

Mercury

573
− 241

Jupiter

937
− 304

Earth

437
− 225

Uranus

968
− 413

397
− 185
I am a ball of rock and metal but covered with soil, rock, and water.

982
− 650
I am a bare, rocky ball similar to Earth's moon.

847
− 214
I am the largest planet in our solar system.

963
− 151
I am surrounded by seven flat rings made of pieces of ice.

857
− 302
I am a planet with 27 known moons.

596
− 323
I am called the Red Planet.

A Place in Space

Draw a line to each matching difference to connect each planet, star, or space object to a fact about it.

Venus $\begin{array}{r} 713 \\ -\ 171 \\ \hline \end{array}$	$\begin{array}{r} 952 \\ -\ 236 \\ \hline \end{array}$ I am a planet with days lasting only 16 hours.
Neptune $\begin{array}{r} 833 \\ -\ 117 \\ \hline \end{array}$	$\begin{array}{r} 857 \\ -\ 469 \\ \hline \end{array}$ I am like a dirty snowball made of dust, ice, and gases.
Sun $\begin{array}{r} 675 \\ -\ 216 \\ \hline \end{array}$	$\begin{array}{r} 612 \\ -\ 428 \\ \hline \end{array}$ I am covered with craters.
Moon $\begin{array}{r} 407 \\ -\ 223 \\ \hline \end{array}$	$\begin{array}{r} 931 \\ -\ 389 \\ \hline \end{array}$ I am sizzling hot with no water.
Comet  $\begin{array}{r} 514 \\ -\ 126 \\ \hline \end{array}$	$\begin{array}{r} 892 \\ -\ 433 \\ \hline \end{array}$ I am the star closest to Earth.

 Complete each pattern. Then tell someone the pattern for each set of numbers.

900, 800, 700, _____, _____, _____, _____, _____, _____

900, 700, 500, _____, _____

800, 600, 400, _____

Tricky Zero

Subtract.

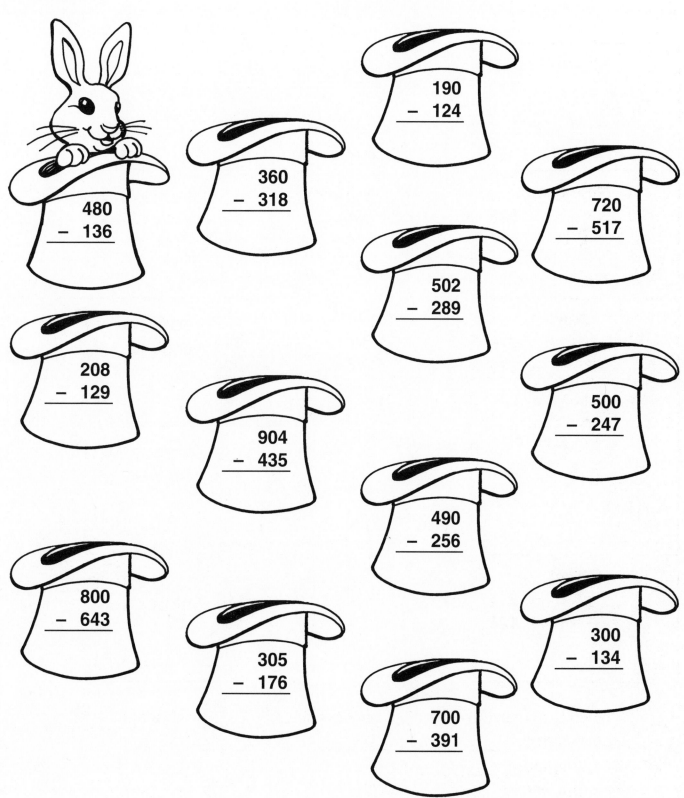

480
− 136

360
− 318

190
− 124

720
− 517

502
− 289

208
− 129

904
− 435

490
− 256

500
− 247

800
− 643

305
− 176

700
− 391

300
− 134

Name _____

Treasures Under the Sea

Add or subtract. Use the chart to color the picture.

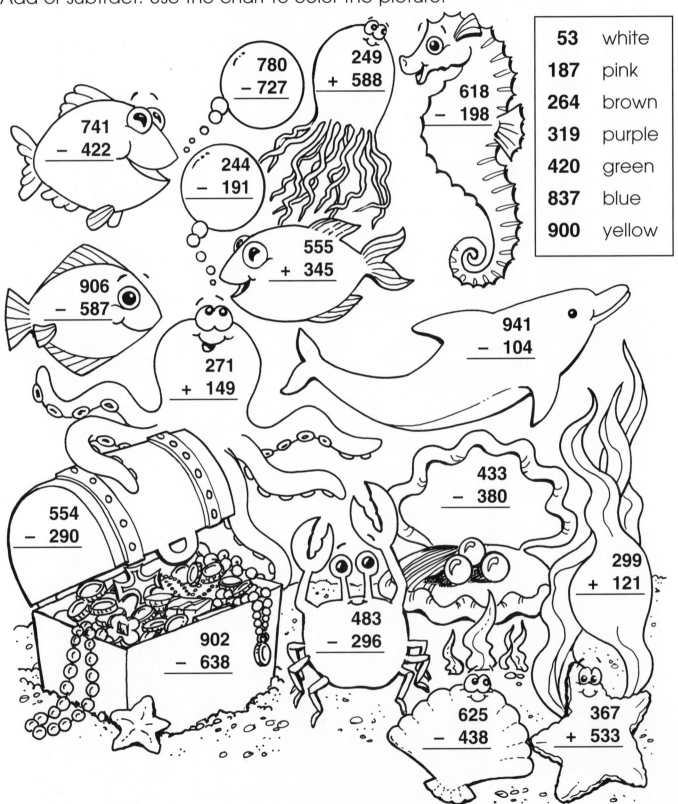

53	white
187	pink
264	brown
319	purple
420	green
837	blue
900	yellow

780 − 727

249 + 588

741 − 422

618 − 198

244 − 191

555 + 345

906 − 587

941 − 104

271 + 149

554 − 290

433 − 380

299 + 121

902 − 638

483 − 296

625 − 438

367 + 533

Follow the Trees

Add or subtract. Then trace the bear's path to its cave. The bear follows trees with sums that have a 3 in the tens place.

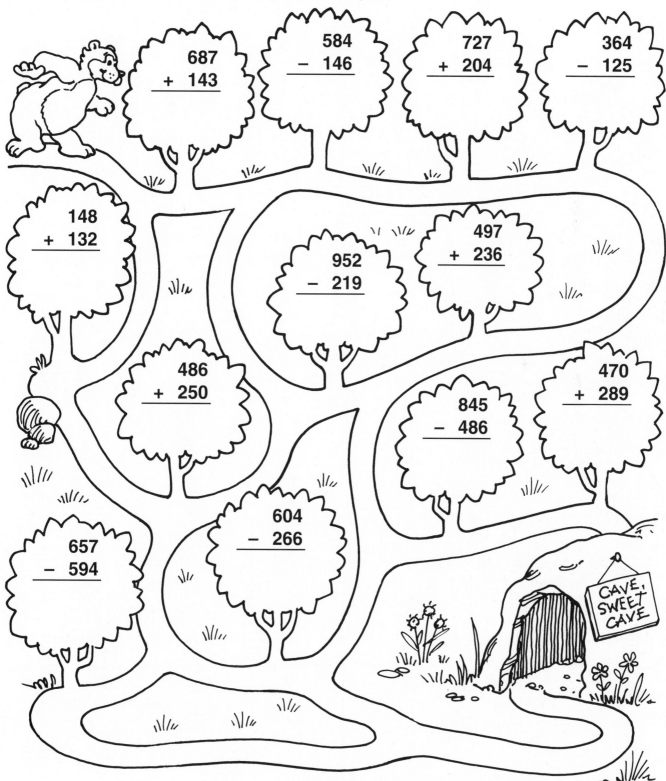

$$687 + 143$$

$$584 - 146$$

$$727 + 204$$

$$364 - 125$$

$$148 + 132$$

$$952 - 219$$

$$497 + 236$$

$$486 + 250$$

$$845 - 486$$

$$470 + 289$$

$$657 - 594$$

$$604 - 266$$

CAVE, SWEET CAVE

School Supplies

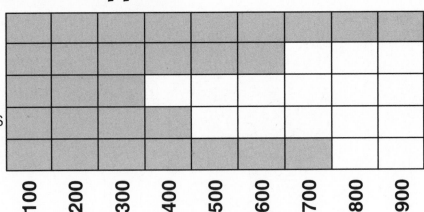

markers
folders
scissors
glue sticks
pencils

100 200 300 400 500 600 700 800 900

Add or subtract. Use the graph to help solve each problem.

A. Mrs. Randolph's class used 523 pencils. How many are left?

B. Mr. Kirk's class used 156 scissors. How many are left?

C. Mr. Dean's class took 248 folders. Mr. Jordan's class took 176 folders. How many did they take altogether?

How many folders are left?

D. Mrs. Fenton's class used 96 glue sticks. Mrs. McBride's class used 189 glue sticks. How many did they use altogether?

How many glue sticks are left?

E. Mrs. Barry's class needs 275 markers. Mr. Lopez's class needs 398 markers. How many do they need altogether?

How many markers are left?

Movie Madness

Add or subtract to solve.

A. 168 people are in line to buy tickets. 159 seats are available in the theater. How many people will not get a ticket to the movie?

B. 427 people attended the rush hour show. 289 people attended the 7:00 show. How many attended both shows altogether?

C. 507 people ordered a popcorn and a soda. 278 people ordered popcorn only. How many more people ordered a soda?

D. 319 people bought a pretzel. 299 people bought a box of candy. How many pretzels and candy were sold altogether?

E. There were 826 people at the movie theater on Friday. On Saturday, there were 697 people. How many more people were at the movie theater on Friday?

F. 258 people ordered a hot dog with mustard. 273 people ordered a hot dog with ketchup. How many hot dogs were ordered in all?

Animal Facts

Add or subtract.

T 247 + 253	**O** 463 + 440	**L** 217 + 68	**P** 639 + 207	**A** 391 + 144	**W** 459 + 492	**I** 198 + 672
P 842 − 314	**L** 504 + 475	**I** 500 − 293	**R** 457 + 364	**I** 903 − 339	**O** 107 + 147	**A** 924 − 71
N 700 − 427	**N** 903 − 34	**R** 703 − 186	**H** 258 + 553	**A** 357 + 537		

Move across each row. Write the letter from each box with the correct number of hundreds.

2 hundreds	I am a cat that likes to sleep 20 hours a day.	▢▢▢▢

5 hundreds	I have four toes on my front feet and three toes on my back feet.	▢▢▢▢▢

8 hundreds	I am a fish with razor-sharp teeth.	▢▢▢▢▢▢▢

9 hundreds	I can see well at night but cannot move my eyes.	▢▢▢

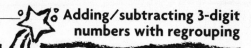
Very Special Helpers

Add or subtract. Write the letter that goes with each answer in the center.

B	E	L	H	F	D	A
207 + 566	814 − 245	339 + 128	540 − 166	422 − 174	615 − 230	409 + 387

N
772
− 484

I
635
+ 199

248　834　800　569　689　796　288

O
596
+ 287

M
841
− 152

896　569　796　259　374　569　800

C
600
− 341

T
478
+ 418

385　883　259　896　883　800

467　834　773　800　796　800　834　796　288

R
603
+ 197

P
416
+ 288

704　883　467　834　259　569　689　796　288

Vacation Time

Write the name and the price of each item in the correct suitcase. Add the prices.

$.77

$7.14

$2.10

$6.89

Beach

$ _____
$ _____
$ _____
$ _____

Total $ _____

$1.23

Mountains

$ _____
$ _____
$ _____
$ _____

Total $ _____

$1.23

$1.46

$3.74

How much more does it cost to fill the mountain suitcase than the beach suitcase? Show your work on another piece of paper.

Bull's-Eye

Select any problem. Add or subtract. Color the answer on the target.
Repeat until you hit the bull's-eye. Then answer the remaining problems.

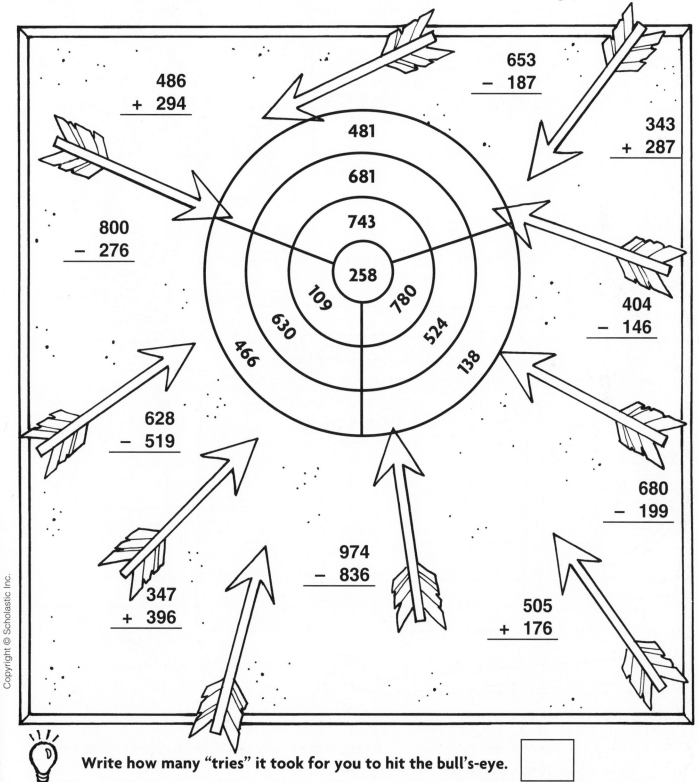

Write how many "tries" it took for you to hit the bull's-eye.

Grid Math

	A	B	C	D
3	550	636	282	963
2	189	148	579	415
1	427	751	370	804

Find the numbers on the grid. Add or subtract.

(A, 1) + (C, 3)

(B, 3) − (A, 3)

(D, 3) − (A, 2)

(B, 2) + (C, 1)

(A, 3) + (C, 1)

(D, 1) − (B, 3)

(A, 2) + (B, 1)

(C, 2) − (C, 3)

(D, 3) − (B, 2)

(D, 2) + (A, 2)

Perfect Punt

Add or subtract. Draw a line to connect
each football to its goalpost.

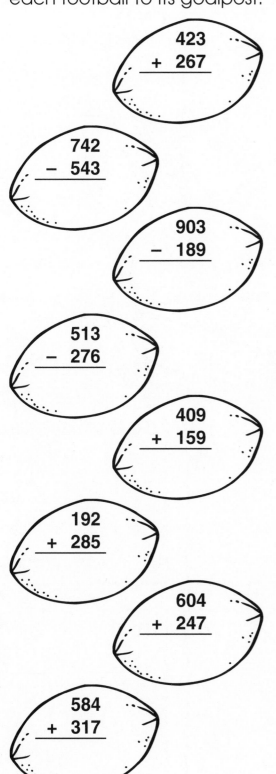

$$423 + 267$$

$$742 - 543$$

$$903 - 189$$

$$513 - 276$$

$$409 + 159$$

$$192 + 285$$

$$604 + 247$$

$$584 + 317$$

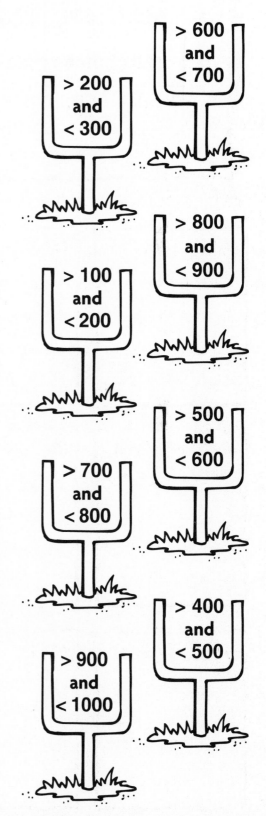

> 200 and < 300

> 600 and < 700

> 800 and < 900

> 100 and < 200

> 500 and < 600

> 700 and < 800

> 400 and < 500

> 900 and < 1000

Tic-Tac-Toe

How to Play:

1. Solve the problems in the first row of a game.

2. Mark the gameboard anywhere with an X or O for the largest answer.

3. Continue to solve the problems. Place an X or O to get three in a row.

Game 1

X	O
374 + 263	429 + 187
154 + 199	740 − 286
643 + 208	341 + 459
973 − 784	514 − 188
291 + 263	445 + 375

Gameboard 1

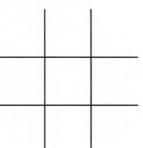

Gameboard 2

Game 2

X	O
166 + 117	149 + 69
801 − 389	722 − 305
318 + 218	266 + 243
576 + 268	607 + 266
629 − 457	785 − 657

Page 4

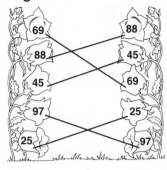

seven, nine

Page 5

Check that the child has drawn the correct number of petals on each flower. Bows with 4, 6, 8, and 10 should be colored yellow. Bows with 3, 5, 7, and 9 should be colored purple.

Page 6

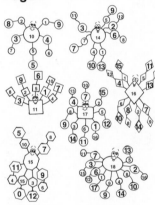

Page 7

A. 3, 2; B. 12, 5; C. 8, 6; D. 11, 7; E. 7, 5; F. 12, 3; G. 4, 1; H. 10, 8; I. 9, 4; J. 11, 5; Answers will vary.

Page 8

21, 93, 78, 46, 44, 78; PLEASE

50, 67, 46, 79, 83, 59, 25, 66; THANK YOU

59, 25, 66, 32, 78; YOU'RE

80, 78, 93, 18, 25, 35, 78; WELCOME

Page 9

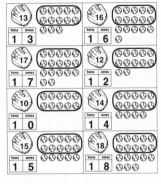

Answers will vary.

Page 10

38, 26, 97, 58, 67, 76, 79; 46, 84, 46, 89, 58, 48, 97; 58, 55, 65, 46, 40; THREE-FOURTHS, PACIFIC

Page 11

62, 33, 23; 30, 21, 14; 61, 22, 41; The bird with the difference of 30 should be colored red. The bird with the difference of 14 should be colored blue. The birds with the differences of 22 and 33 should be colored green.

Page 12

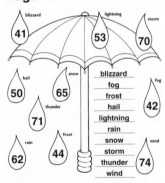

Page 13

54, 85, 43, 85; 43, 54, 67; 43, 67, 32; 32; Check child's coloring.

Page 14

10, 12, 16; 18, 14, 19; 15, 11, 17; Bowls with 11, 15, and 18 should be colored yellow. Bowls with 10, 14, and 17 should be colored pink. Bowls with 12, 16, and 19 should be colored brown.

Page 15

tens	ones
1	3

tens	ones
1	6

tens	ones
1	7

tens	ones
1	2

tens	ones
1	0

tens	ones
1	4

tens	ones
1	5

tens	ones
1	8

Page 16

A. 52, 93, 72, 93; B. 41, 62, 37, 37; C. 23, 50, 62, 62; D. 60, 32, 81, 60; E. 90, 44, 76, 44

Page 17

71	93	90	52
92	90	91	86	92
81	81	73	42	92
85	74	92	90	94
51	41	93	81

Page 18

Beach: Route #1—13 + 48 + 32 + 54 = 147 miles; Route #2—13 + 48 + 88 + 39 = 188 miles

Mountains: Route #1—13 + 17 + 31 + 49 = 110 miles; Route #2—13 + 28 + 10 + 25 = 76 miles

Page 19

35: 3 tens 5 ones, 2 tens 15 ones; 47: 4 tens 7 ones, 3 tens 17 ones; 82: 8 tens 2 ones, 7 tens 12 ones; 94: 9 tens 4 ones, 8 tens 14 ones; 61: 6 tens 1 one, 5 tens 11 ones; 90: 9 tens 0 ones, 8 tens 10 ones

Page 20

Boldfaced numbers should be circled.

A. **48**, 89; B. 79, **46**; C. 36, **76**; D. **77**, 59; E. **48**, 14; F. 61, **68**; G. 14, **39**; Answers will vary.

Page 21

A. 19, 39, 37; 1, 3, 2; B. 8, 6, 9; 2, 1, 3; C. 28, 37, 14; 2, 3, 1; D. 29, 38, 37; 1, 3, 2; E. 29, 36, 48; 1, 2, 3; F. 18, 15, 19; 2, 1, 3

Page 22

65 − 27 = 38, 38 + 27 = 65; 77 − 38 = 39, 39 + 38 = 77; 24 − 15 = 9, 9 + 15 = 24; 32 − 13 = 19, 19 + 13 = 32; 83 − 49 = 34, 34 + 49 = 83; 50 − 19 = 31, 31 + 19 = 50; 46 − 29 = 17, 17 + 29 = 46; 62 − 15 = 47, 47 + 15 = 62

Answers will vary.

Page 23

U. 81; L. 5; N. 60; C. 46; O. 90; P. 38; H. 23; K. 63; S. 48; A. 14; G. 18; M. 71; R. 69; KANGAROO; KOALA; OPOSSUM; POUCH

Page 24

Check that the child has colored the appropriate spaces. A. 21; B. 9; C. 26; D. 8; E. 13; F. 17; G. 30; H. 7

Page 25

A. 28 + 25 = 53; B. 25 − 9 = 16; C. 28 − 13 = 15; D. 12 + 9 = 21; E. 12 − 9 = 3; F. 13 + 28 = 41; G. 9 + 25 + 12 = 46; 98 students

Page 26

saw: 34 + 27 + 5 = 66; wrench: 48 + 36 + 15 = 99; hammer: 43 + 15 + 27 = 85; pliers: 39 + 34 + 15 = 88; A. 27 + 15 = 42; B. 34 − 5 = 29, 48 − 15 = 33; 43 − 15 = 28; 39 − 15 = 24; 43 + 15 + 27 + 5 + 34 + 39 + 48 + 15 + 36 = 262

Page 27

A. 596, red; B. 995, blue; C. 877, blue; D. 569, blue; E. 662, red; F. 978, red; G. 968, red; H. 596, red; I. 899, blue; J. 497, blue

Page 28

2 hundreds 7 tens;
8 hundreds 4 tens;
9 hundreds 3 tens;
7 hundreds 1 ten;
5 hundreds 6 tens;
3 hundreds 2 tens;
4 hundreds 9 tens;
6 hundreds 5 tens;
570; 804

Page 29

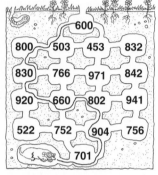

Problems will vary.

Page 30

A. $1.49 + $.50 + $.75 + $1.22 = $3.96; B. $1.72 + $.65 + $1.17 = $3.54; C. $1.86 + $1.84 + $.84 + $1.07 = $5.61; D. $1.53 + $1.90 + $1.22 + $.84 = $5.49; E. $1.86 + $.50 + $1.17 = $3.53; F. $1.49 + $.86 + $.75 = $3.10

Page 31

A. 123 + 406 + 406 = 935, orange; B. 209 + 81 + 147 + 181 + 72 = 690, green; C. 146 + 266 + 120 + 139 + 82 = 753, purple; D. 180 + 169 + 308 + 122 = 779, yellow; E. 154 + 154 + 188 + 93 + 82 + 170 = 841, red; F. 107 + 173 + 38 + 280 + 38 + 54 + 78 = 768, blue

Page 32

40 tens, 20 tens, 70 tens, 50 tens; 10 tens, 90 tens, 80 tens, 30 tens

Page 33

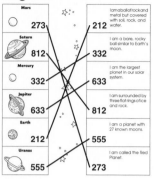

Page 34

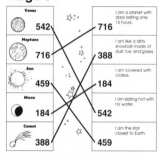

900, 800, 700, 600, 500, 400, 300, 200, 100, Subtract 100.; 900, 700, 500, 300, 100, Subtract 200.; 800, 600, 400, 200, Subtract 200.

Page 35

Page 36

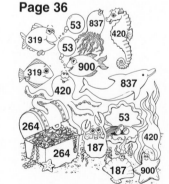

Check child's coloring.

Page 37

Page 38

A. 700 − 523 = 177; B. 300 − 156 = 144; C. 248 + 176 = 424, 600 − 424 = 176; D. 189 + 96 = 285, 400 − 285 = 115; E. 398 + 275 = 673, 900 − 673 = 227

Page 39

A. 168 − 159 = 9; B. 427 + 289 = 716; C. 507 − 278 = 229; D. 319 + 299 = 618; E. 826 − 697 = 129; F. 258 + 273 = 531

Page 40

T. 500; O. 903; L. 285; P. 846; A. 535; W. 951; I. 870; P. 528; L. 979; I. 207; R. 821; I. 564; O. 254; A. 853; N. 273; N. 869; R. 517; H. 811; A. 894; LION, TAPIR, PIRANHA, OWL

Page 41

B. 773; E. 569; L. 467; H. 374; F. 248; D. 385; A. 796; N. 288; I. 834; O. 883; M. 689; C. 259; T. 896; R. 800; P. 704; FIREMAN, TEACHER, DOCTOR, LIBRARIAN, POLICEMAN

Page 42

sandals $2.10 + swimsuits $6.89 + sand toys $1.23 + swim ring $1.46 = $11.68

mittens $.77 + coat $7.14 + hat $1.23 + skis $3.74 = $12.88

$12.88 − $11.68 = $1.20

Page 43

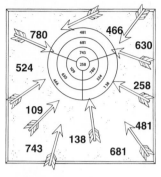

Answers will vary.

Page 44

427 + 282 = 709;
636 − 550 = 86;
963 − 189 = 774;
148 + 370 = 518;
550 + 370 = 920;
804 − 636 = 168;
189 + 751 = 940;
579 − 282 = 297;
963 − 148 = 815;
415 + 189 = 604

Page 45

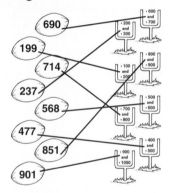

Page 46

Game 1: 637, 616; 353, 454; 851, 800; 189, 326; 554, 820

Game 2: 283, 218; 412, 417; 536, 509; 844, 873; 172, 128